MW01154945

Nature's Neighborhoods
All About Ecosystems

Welcome to the City at Night

by Ruth Owen

Ruby Tuesday Books

Published in 2024 by Ruby Tuesday Books Ltd.

Copyright © 2024 Ruby Tuesday Books Ltd.

All rights reserved. No part of this publication may be reproduced in whole or in part, stored in any retrieval system, or transmitted in any form or by any means, electronic, mechanical, photocopying, recording, or otherwise, without written permission from the publisher.

Editor: Ruth Owen
Design and Production: Alix Wood

Photo credits
Nature Picture Library: 5 (Stephen Dalton), 7 (Luke Massey), 8 (Charlie Hamilton-Brown), 9 (Ernie Janes), 11 (Laurent Geslin), 12 (Terry Whittaker), 13 (Michael Durham), 17B (Adrian Davies), 19R (Kim Taylor), 21 (Klaus Echle), 25L (Nigel Cattlin), 25R (Ingo Arndt), 27 (Klein & Hubert), 28B (Stephen Dalton), 29 (Matthew Maran); Shutterstock: Cover (Anton Vierietin/Photo Art Wall Decoration), 2 (Eric Isselee), 3 (Harry Collins Photography/ Josep Curto/stockphoto mania/Krisana Antharith), 4L (Andrzej Rostek), 4TR (BonNontawat), 4BR (Farts Pfotografy), 6L (Smiler99), 6R (Ryan DeBerardinis/Protasov AN), 10T (Takamon), 10B (Phakamat BL), 14–15 (Evgenii Emelianov), 15T (Marta Fernandez Jimenez), 16 (Bildagentur Zoonar GmbH), 17T (Vita Serendipity), 18L (Lee Hua Ming), 18R (DimaBerlin), 19 (Martin Janca), 22 (Kyle Moore), 23 (Steve Midgley), 24L (Lisa-S), 24R (Zebra Studio), 26T (PJ Photography), 26B (Eric Isselee), 28T (artfotoxyz), 30, 31TL (Dmytro Leschenko), 31BL, (Richard Hadfield), 31TR (Richard Thornton), 31BR (Vladimir Mulder), 32 (Eric Isselee/Pakhnyushchy); Superstock: 20 (Jamie Hall/Frank Lane Picture Agency).

Library of Congress Control Number: 2023903517
Print (Hardback) ISBN 978-1-78856-299-7
Print (Paperback) ISBN 978-1-78856-300-0
eBook PDF ISBN 978-1-78856-301-7
ePub ISBN 978-1-78856-302-4

Published in Minneapolis, MN
Printed in the United States

www.rubytuesdaybooks.com

Contents

Words shown in **bold** in the text
are explained in the glossary.

Welcome to the City at Night

A city **habitat** can be home to animals and to plants, such as grass and trees.

We might not always see the animals, but they are there.

Stadium lights

Insects

Raccoon

GARBAGE

BAGE

Slug eggs

Many of the animals are **nocturnal** and only come out at night.

The plants and animals in this habitat get everything they need to survive from the city.

A city is a type of ecosystem. An ecosystem includes all the living things in an area. It also includes non-living things such as rain, buildings, and even trash cans. Everything in an ecosystem has its own part to play.

Red fox

Let's find out what happens when darkness falls. Welcome to the night-time city!

A Rooftop Hunter

The Sun is setting on a city. Pigeons fly up to their night-time **roosts** on high window ledges.

But someone is watching them.

Suddenly, a peregrine falcon dives from a tall building.

Pigeon

A peregrine falcon diving

In a full stoop, or dive, the falcon can fly at 200 miles (320 km) per hour!

She slams into a pigeon with her feet, killing it instantly.

Then she carries it back to her chicks in the family's rooftop nest.

Mother peregrine falcon

Peregrine falcons build nests on steep cliffs. But some of them have become city **dwellers**. In a city, there are high places to nest and plenty of pigeons to hunt.

Chick

Which nocturnal animals live beneath a city's streets?

Let's Have Takeout!

Far below the falcon's nest, a family of rats climbs from its underground home.

These **urban** animals like to stay hidden from people.

They live under the city streets in the **sewers** and drains.

Rat

Rats are clever animals with a very good sense of smell.

At night, they sniff out food in the trash containers close to restaurants.

Rats are **omnivores.** This means they eat meat and fruits and vegetables. City rats find lots of human leftovers to feed on.

Which speedy insects will share the rats' garbage can feast?

Hungry Cockroaches

Fast-moving cockroaches scuttle from a storm drain.

They climb over the trash, feeding on the human leftovers.

They will eat almost anything—even the rats' poop!

Cockroaches inside a drain

Cockroach

Cockroaches are nocturnal insects. They like **moisture** and the dark, so they live in drains and pipes.

Sniff. Sniff. A hungry vixen, or female fox, creeps toward the trash.

The rats scurry away because they don't want to become a fox's dinner.

The vixen laps up some rainwater, and then she grabs a burger and disappears into the darkness.

Fox

Storm drain

Rainwater

What do you think foxes do all night?

Busy Scavengers

Foxes spend the night hunting for mice, voles, rats, and birds.

They are also **scavengers** that will feed on trash and the bodies of dead animals.

If a fox finds more food than it can eat or carry, it buries the spare food—often in a backyard! Then, the fox returns to dig up and eat its buried meal another night.

Fox

Raccoons are smart city scavengers that will also sniff out trash to eat.

Sometimes, they balance on a garbage can until it topples over.

They may even use their hand-like front paws to open latches on the lids of trash containers!

A raccoon's main food is fruits, nuts, insects, eggs, frogs, fish, and mice.

Raccoon

Which tall park dwellers have been busy all day keeping the air clean?

A Safe Place to Sleep

Trees that grow in city parks help clean the air.

All day, cars, buses, and delivery vans puff out harmful carbon dioxide gas.

The trees use their leaves to take this gas from the air.

Trees use sunlight, water, and carbon dioxide to make sugary, energy-giving food in their leaves. As they do this, they also make oxygen that people and animals need to breathe.

Sparrow

At night, the trees have another important job to do.

Daytime birds such as sparrows roost on their branches and huddle in cracks in the trees' trunks.

The trees keep the sleeping birds safe from foxes, rats, and pet cats.

Which flying insects hide on the trunks of trees and wait for night to fall?

Flying at Night

During the day in spring and summer, lime hawkmoths shelter in the trees in some city parks.

At night, they take to the air to **mate**.

After mating, the females lay their eggs on the leaves of the trees.

Female lime hawkmoth

Male lime hawkmoth

Caterpillars hatch from the eggs and feed on the trees' leaves.

Lime hawkmoth caterpillar

Lime hawkmoths only eat when they are caterpillars. The adult moths live for just a few weeks and don't feed during this time.

Pupa

Once it's ready to become a **pupa**, a caterpillar climbs down from its tree and buries itself in soil.

Next spring, the pupa will become an adult moth.

Which nocturnal city dwellers have gone to a soccer game?

17

In the Spotlight

Inside city parks, soccer games are played at night under floodlights.

Thousands of nocturnal flying insects are attracted to the bright lights.

A cloud of moths, mosquitoes, and little flies, known as gnats and midges, is good news for other park residents—bats!

A midge fly

A midge is about the size of a grain of sugar.

A brown long-eared bat swoops from the trees and grabs a moth.

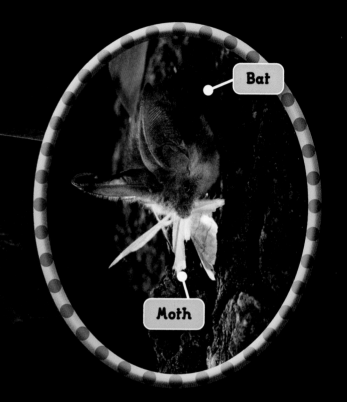

Bat

Moth

Brown long-eared bat

Brown long-eared bats weigh the same as a large grape. By day, they roost in trees and in the attics of houses.

Then it flies to a tree trunk and hangs upside-down to eat its meal.

Who is visiting city gardens to find lush, green grass to eat?

Silent Visitors

It's past midnight. Slowly and silently, deer appear from wooded places at the edge of a city.

They move from one yard to another, feeding on lawns.

Humans are part of a city ecosystem, too. Our gardens provide shelter, water, and food for wild animals. Our garbage cans are also a source of food.

The vixen is still looking for food.

She jumps into a backyard, easily climbing over a fence that's 6 feet (2 m) high.

She helps herself to some food and water that's been left out for a pet cat.

Then she poops and pees on the deck.

This will tell other foxes that this backyard is part of her **territory**.

Why has the fox dug a den beneath a greenhouse?

A Backyard Den

The fox squeezes into the den that she's dug in the soil beneath a greenhouse.

In her den, the fox gave birth to four tiny, blind, and deaf cubs.

At first, she stayed with the cubs day and night, and her mate brought her food.

Now the cubs are eight weeks old, and she leaves them at night to go hunting.

The cubs play outside the den and catch worms and insects to eat.

Just like our pet dogs, foxes love to play with things they find. They often steal shoes, gardening gloves, clothes from washing lines, balls, and other toys from gardens!

Eight-week-old fox cubs

Which slimy night-time minibeasts are feeding on plants in backyards?

The Night-Time Slime-Inators

The lettuces, cabbages, and strawberries that people grow in their backyards are a favorite food of snails and slugs.

Snail

Muscular foot

Slug

The slug's eyes are on these tentacles.

The slug breathes through this hole.

The underside of a slug or snail's body is a strong, muscular foot.

To move, it tightens and loosens the muscles and slides along on a trail of slime.

All slugs are both male and female.

After two slugs mate, they can each lay up to 400 eggs.

A tiny baby slug hatches from each egg and immediately starts munching!

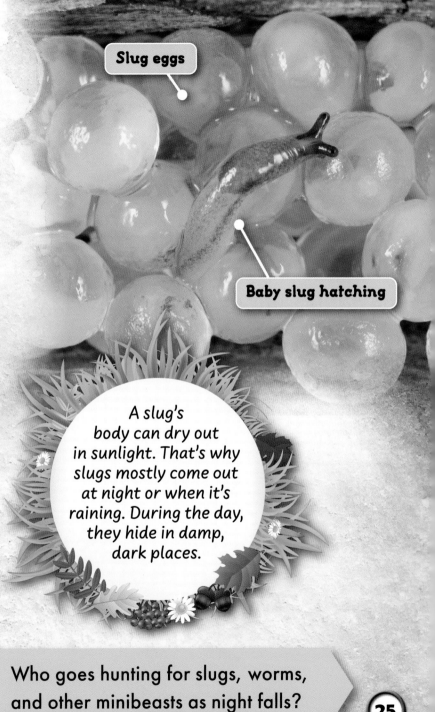

Slug eggs

Baby slug hatching

Slug slime

A slug's body can dry out in sunlight. That's why slugs mostly come out at night or when it's raining. During the day, they hide in damp, dark places.

Who goes hunting for slugs, worms, and other minibeasts as night falls?

25

The Spiky Gang

In the UK and some other parts of Europe, hedgehogs make their homes in cities.

When darkness falls, they **forage** in gardens for slugs, worms, beetles, caterpillars, and other minibeasts.

A hedgehog has 6,000 spines.

Mother hedgehog

Four-day-old hoglet

Female hedgehogs often give birth to their hoglets beneath garden sheds. Once they are three weeks old, the hoglets go foraging with their mother at night.

A hedgehog may roam around an area the size of 30 soccer fields looking for food.

In one night it might walk for more than a mile (1.6 km)!

It may even swim across garden ponds to find food.

Who is bringing home some food to the fox family's den?

It's Morning!

As the Sun rises, the night-time animals head back to their homes and hiding places.

A rat has been foraging for food in a backyard compost heap.

Now, she hurries back to the nest she dug in the soil beneath the compost heap.

Rat

A rat gives birth to up to 10 pups at one time. The female pups are ready to mate and have babies when they are about 10 weeks old.

Rat pup

Vixen

Male, or dog, fox

Rat

But one rat has not made it home as the new day begins.

The vixen's mate returns to his family with a rat he caught on a city street.

All day, the nocturnal animals will hide. But when darkness falls, the night-time city will come alive again.

29

A Night-Time City Food Web

A food web shows who eats who in a habitat.

This food web shows the connections between some of the living things in a city.

Plants can make the food they need for energy inside themselves. To do this, they need sunlight.

Peregrine falcon

Fox

Rat

Pigeon

Plants

Hedgehog

The arrows mean: **eaten by**

Garbage

Slug

Glossary

dweller
A person or animal that lives in a specific place.

forage
To search for food in the area where you live.

habitat
The place where a living thing, such as a plant or animal, makes its home. Gardens, parks, and woodlands are all types of habitats.

mate
An animal's partner with which it has young; also the word for when two animals get together to produce young.

moisture
A small amount of water.

nocturnal
Only active at night.

omnivore
An animal that eats both plants and other animals.

pupa
The stage in an insect's life between being a larva and becoming an adult.

roost
The place where a bird regularly rests or sleeps.

scavenger
An animal that feeds on dead bodies or plants, and garbage.

sewer
An underground pipe that carries waste from toilets, sinks, baths, and showers to a place where it can be treated.

territory
The place where an animal lives and finds its food and mates.

urban
From a town or city.

Index